Hip. Hip. Hallelujah!
DR. JOHN DEE JEFFRIES
EDITED BY C. GENEVIEVE JEFFRIES
Author of The Last Martyr; and, When I Can't Find God
VOLUME 1

PUBLISHED *by* PARABLES
Earthly Stories with a Heavenly Meaning

Hip. Hip. Hallelujah! Volume 1
Copyright © John Dee Jeffries
Author of Hip. Hip. Hallelujah, Volume 1, 2, & 3,
The Last Martyr; and, When I Can't Find God

Published By Parables

All Rights Reserved. No part of this book may be reproduced or utilized in any form or by any means, electronic or mechanical, including photocopying, recording, or by any information storage and retrieval system, without permission in writing from the author.

Unless otherwise specified Scripture quotations are taken from the authorized version of the King James Bible.

First Edition   June, 2017

ISBN 978-1-945698-34-7

Printed in the United States of America

Readers should be aware that Internet Web sites offered as citations and/or sources for further information may have been changed or disappeared between the time this was written and when it is read.

Illustration provided by www.unsplash.com

Hip, Hip, Hallelujah!
DR. JOHN DEE JEFFRIES
EDITED BY C. GENEVIEVE JEFFRIES
Author of The Last Martyr; and, When I Can't Find God
VOLUME 1

PUBLISHED *by* PARABLES
Earthly Stories with a Heavenly Meaning

Preface
Life Shouldn't Just Happen!

Do you ever wish life had a "redo" feature? My word process has one. If I make a typographical error I can use the "redo" feature to "undo" the mistakes I've made! If something goes awry, I just use the "redo" feature.

Do you ever wish life had a "redo" feature?

My computer has a "restore" feature too! If things get so terribly messed up I can use the "restore" feature to take my computer backward in time to a time before things got messed up.

Do you ever wish life had a "restore" feature?

When I was younger I used to play golf. I wasn't much of a golfer. Sometimes the ball would fly this way, sometimes that way and, more often than not – simply go astray! A "mulligan!" A "mulligan" carries the same idea as the "redo" and "restore" features on the computer. You get a second chance! You disregard the errant shot! No penalties! No consequences! Simply take the shot over!

Do you ever wish life would give you a "mulligan?"

I think all of us can look backward with regret – over things we've done or over things we've said. And, we wish life would provide a "redo" feature, or a "restore" feature – we wish life would give us a "mulligan!"

Bad News -- Life doesn't work that way!
Good News –God Does!

God is the God of second chances! God, through the work of Jesus Christ on the Cross not only forgives our sins -- He actually "cancels" our past!

Many people struggle to move forward in life! At some point they seem to make forward progress! Then, inexplicably, the long arm of the past grabs them and pulls them backward! They're suddenly overwhelmed and stymied by feelings of embarrassment! Deep feelings of guilt, shame, regret and more stubbornly appear! These dark feelings rush to the surface – people are snarled, trapped, shattered – and stuck!

> Into our *Shattered* Lives
> Jesus "restores" our Hearts!
>
> Into our *Shattered* Families
> Jesus "restores' our Homes!
>
> Into our *Shattered* World
> Jesus "restores" our Hope!

> "Comes a time, on the journey,
> You wonder how you will survive,
> There comes a time,
> When you're thirsty and so alone...
> There is a pool in the desert,
> Where water flows from fountains unseen,
> Saving water, Healing water
> flowing over me."
> The Choir, Flowing Over Me --
> Flap Your Wings

When we look backward at some of the situations we've been involved in and some of the choices we've made, we think, if only I had a second chance. Sometimes when we make a mistake in life it feels so final, you may think it's all over for you; but, know this – God is a God who provides that much needed second chance.

There's a new day coming! Our past failures are not final and our pain need not be fatal!

Know this -- your yesterdays don't always have to determine your tomorrows!

Hip. Hip.
Hallelujah!
Now where's my golf club?

A Vital Question
Are these stories true?

Yes! Double-Yes! Triple-Yes! But, remember, we are commanded to "speak the truth -- in love!" Each of these stories are true! Definitely! They really did happen! However, they are told with "love" – by that I mean that the identity of the innocent and the guilty -- are protected! No need to "shoot the wounded." No need to "tar and feather" those who have stumbled, slipped, and fallen! Each of these stories are true! Definitely! They really did happen! However, once again, remember, they are told with "love."

In the aftermath of hurricane Katrina I traveled across the nation, speaking before large and small groups of people, in large and small churches -- pleading for God's church

-- the broken body of Christ in St. Bernard parish, Louisiana. A pastor in a church in Oklahoma where I spoke said, "John, I've never been so encouraged by such a discouraging message!"

Imagine That! The Discouraged Encouraged by Discouragement!

For me, hurricane Katrina was one of the most discouraging events I'd ever encountered. For the first time in American history – an entire parish (county) was completely destroyed. We're not talking about one town or one city – we're talking about every building (business, school, church, home, everything) in the ENTIRE parish or county (not just a part of it). Everything and Everyone (63,000 population in St. Bernard parish) were displaced. Less than two months later, living nearly 90 miles away near Baton Rouge, Louisiana, my wife was afflicted by a brain aneurism, followed by emergency brain surgery, followed by a post-operative stroke!

A pastor friend, Bill Hild, First Baptist Church, Sarasota, Florida when hearing of our plight visited with me via telephone. "John," says he, "Know this, every miracle in the Bible began with someone in a mess! You're in a mess, John, and a prime candidate for a miracle!

Hip. Hip. Hallelujah! The miracles came!

I developed a habit of saying that "I've seen more miracles and miraculous movements of God in the aftermath of hurricane Katrina than I had in all my years of ministry before Katrina!"

Then, God tapped me on the shoulder and said, "Wait a minute!"

Since that time God has been showing me how He has been and is moving and ministering through all the years of the circumstances of my life – even before I entered full-time ministry!

> My ministry has been full – full of God – full of God – full of God!
> Hip. Hip. Hallelujah!

Sometimes, faith dwindled and I placed limitations on God (Psalm 78:41 & Mark 6:5). This was and is, however, a profound mistake. God's power has no limitations and He can work mighty miracles in my life and in your life – if we let Him!

Something else. In old Jerusalem, several winding streets serve as a market place. It was in a market place that Jeremiah saw a skilled craftsman, a potter, making a vessel of clay. In the midst of Jeremiah's observing the potter do his thing – God did a God thing! God spoke to Jeremiah – gave him revelation and a deeper glimpse of truth. Now, here's the kicker – perhaps as many as a thousand people saw that potter. Jeremiah saw God! Hip. Hip. Hallelujah!

I hope you see God in these stories! Each of these stories are true! Definitely! They really did happen!

By the way, in the Bible, when God does His thing, we call them "miracles" – today, people call them "God Things" ("God Things" are when God does something miraculous).

I call them "God's Kisses" – hey, listen, as I write this I have Divine Lipstick smeared all over me! No kidding! And so do you! Nothing can separate me and nothing can separate you from the love of God! True stories – "truth spoken in love!"

Hip! Hip! Hallelujah!

May God kiss you through these stories – even as He has kissed me! Now, what's that smudge of red on your cheek.

2nd verse, same as the first --
Hip! Hip! Hallelujah!

An Unspeakable Opportunity!
"Put your hands behind your back!"

Like a runner at the starting block he was filled with eager anticipation. It was day one and his ministry had just begun. Everyone was amazed! The amount of work that young man accomplished – simply amazing! But, something was wrong.

He had forces working within him – that were driving him to do more and more and more! He was striving for approval, driven by feelings of inferiority, low self-image, low self-esteem and more!

Then, when he couldn't keep up he took little pills to get up –uppers! Up! Up! Up! Buy only a few! Only a few! Do more! Do more! Buy! Buy! Buy! Take More! Do More! Buy! Buy! Buy! Sell to buy! Sell! Sell! Sell! More! More! More! Buy! What....?

"Put your hands behind your back!"

What? Prison! Getting up brought him down! Lost it all… Lost his marriage… Lost his family… Lost his ministry… Lost it all! Beware! Be Aware!

Let's make a deal. Since today really is the first day of the rest of your life – let's live like it. Lets live today and the days that follow with eager anticipation. OK. Thanks for making the deal. Now…

Like a runner at the starting block you are probably filled with eager anticipation. It is day one! A new journey has just begun and you're off and running. Be assured, the race you are now running is laden with unspeakable opportunity -- and challenges. Blessings multiplied await the diligent. You're on a faith journey, running with patience the race that is before you (Hebrews 12:1).

Beside you, with you, and for you is a "friend who sticks closer than a brother" (Proverbs 18:24). Jesus is that Friend. He will guide you through this journey to delightful shores which yesterday seemed a distant dream. In the running of this race you are not alone. Jesus is running patiently with you, beside you, blazing a new trail for you – because He loves and cares for you.

So run, but do not rush nor be frantic in your efforts. So many feel they are not making progress unless they are swiftly, speedily, and frantically forging head.

Remember, a falling star races through the evening sky, burns brightly, yet with it's great haste proceeds to burn itself out -- to its own destruction!

Today is the day you put your hand to the plow. New furrows are being prepared within your heart by the Holy Spirit to enable you to receive the good seed of the Word of God. Remember, however, that the fruit of our labor ripens slowly. So, be patient. In the running of this race the diligent reap an abundant harvest through patience.

Haste, like a strangling weed, will choke the good seed that is to be sown and imprison your future. There are no short-cuts, nor are there quick solutions. He who is beside you, with you and for you is in no hurry!

So run, but with patience, and pray that you will yield to the wisdom of His guidance and the loving direction of His Spirit.

>   I am praying for you. – John
>   Hip! Hip! Hallelujah!

Resolution One:
>I will live for God.

Resolution Two:
>If no one else does, I still will.
>>-- Jonathan Edwards

Look not back on yesterday
So full of failure and regret'
Look ahead and seek God's way --
All sin confessed you must forget.
   -- Dennis DeHaan, RBC Ministries

The Skill Of Spiritual Discernment
Understanding And Knowing

Haste, is like a strangling weed!

So too is its opposite – procrastination! Both will choke the good seed that is to be sown and imprison your future.

"He that is hasty is a fool!" (Proverbs 14:29). On the other hand "the soul of the sluggard (the procrastinator) craves and gets nothing (Proverbs 13:4).

There's a thin line of separation between haste and procrastination – both can be Trojan Horses – misleading, subversive practices of spiritual deception and spiritual infiltration.

If you fail to distinguish between the two – Spiritual Discernment -- you will have failed at the very thing God has called you to do – "Prove all things; hold fast to that which is good" (2 Thessalonians 5:21)

Two key words are found in Scripture pertaining to Spiritual Discernment. The Old Testament uses the Hebrew word *blyn* while the New Testament uses the Greek word *diakrino*. *Blyn* is used 247 times in the Old Testament and means to discern, to distinguish, or to understand. It has the idea of being able to separate or put space between things. In other words, there are some things that you cannot mix. For instance, you cannot mix and mingle the world and the church, the flesh with the Spirit, the things of God with the things not of God. You cannot mix these two things differing things together. They are incompatible. They simply do not mix.

Spiritual Discernment, in this sense, means that the one who discerns is separating two unmixable realities. This is what Spiritual Discernment is – it is a Spiritual Process – a separation process which separates one thing from another thing because they are different and a distinction must be made between the two. Spiritual Discernment is the skill of understanding and knowing the difference. It is a process of separating that which is from God from that which is not.

The New Testament Greek term – *diakrino* – also means to separate. It is often translated as to judge. What is a Judge's responsibility? A Judge gathers massive amounts of information, sorts through the information, and separates truth from error. He separates truth from untruth. A Judge discerns – engages in this separation process – so that he can make a judgment and render a decision.

In like manner, Spiritual Discernment is the skill of understanding and knowing God's truth. It is a process of separating that which is from God from that which is not! It is the ability to know "that perfect, good and acceptable will of God" (Romans 12:2). Spiritual Discernment is what Paul was referring to in Colossians 1:9 when he wrote – "I want you to be filled with the knowledge of His will in all spiritual wisdom and understanding so you can walk worthy."

God is saying (through the pen of Paul) – "I want you to know my will. I want you to be filled with the knowledge of my will. I want you to discern the truth of everything – absolutely everything – so that you can make spiritual judgments – spiritual decisions! I want you to separate that which is from me from that which is not! Then, under the leadership of my Spirit, through the guidance of my Word --discern and make decisions -- and "run with patience the race that is before you!"

Happy First Day Of The Rest Of Your Life

"He that believeth shall not make haste!"
Proverb 28:16

Haste makes waste!
When you get Impatient, you get Impulsive!

"If you're running a 26-mile marathon, remember that every mile is run one step at a time. If you are writing a book, do it one page at a time. If you're trying to master a new language, try it one word at a time. There are 365 days in the average year. Divide any project by 365 and you'll find that no job is all that intimidating.
-- Charles (Chuck) Swindoll
Insights For Living

"And We Know…."
The Process Of Spiritual Discernment

We're not saved to be defeated! God didn't create us to limp through life! Victory is the expectation God has for every believer. God has saved us to be over comers! Conquerors! Victors! This is our birthright as members of God's family!

God saved us to experience Victory Over Self! Victory Over Sin! and Victory Over Satan! But, what about Victory Over Situations – especially the unchangeable kind! What about victory over circumstances that are beyond our ability to control?

There are basically two types of circumstances: (1) Those which we can control;

and, (2) Those which we cannot. Being a Christian does not grant us immunity from either type. Nor does victory in Jesus elevate us above some of the more dire circumstances of life.

A few years ago a popular song was titled "Bridge Over Troubled Waters." Someone in the Christian community "Christianized" that song by altering the lyrics to indicate that Jesus was the "Bridge" over troubled waters. It was a beautiful song – but it was theologically incorrect!

Jesus is not a "Bridge" over troubled waters. Jesus is our Pathway THROUGH troubled waters. Remember, Jesus said, "I am the Way…" [the Pathway!] He will make away when there is no way – He is our Pathway through troubled waters!

There are some circumstances we hate to go home to, but we must! We would give anything to change these circumstances – but we can't! We have prayed and prayed for God to change our circumstances – but He hasn't!

Think about several one-word descriptions that describe how people that you know approach the unchangeable circumstances of life. If it will help you focus, write the descriptions down. (Hint: Some approach unchangeable circumstances with Anger, for others its Fear, or Anxiety, or Despair, etc). With which of these one-word descriptions do YOU most identify? Why?

Next, take courage from Romans 8:28 – "And we know that all things work together for good to them that love God, to them who are the called according to his purpose."

Notice the word "know" – Paul is saying he "knows" based on prior experience with God. The knowledge that he has wasn't learned in a book, but through and by personal experience with God. Notice that Paul also says – "….we know…." We – all of us -- gain this kind of knowledge in the same way – through experience, personal experience with God. That kind of experience, personel experience with God, gives us the kind of knowledge that Paul is writing about – the kind that gives us a certain sense of certitude, confidence, and conviction as we forge ahead through both changeable and unchangeable circumstances!

Take heart, you're on that road, the road less traveled, the road that leads through both changeable and unchangeable circumstances. Allow God to create in you that certain sense of certitude, confidence, and conviction as you continue your life journey with Him.

Notice also that "God works ALL things together for GOOD…" Paul is not saying that all things are GOOD in and of themselves. He does say, however, that God is "working" ALL things – even the uncomfortable things, even the not-so-good things, even the unchangeable things of life – He is working ALL together for GOOD -- your good!

Hide this thought in your heart for a rainy day – When everything seems like it's falling apart, that's when God is putting things together, bringing order out of disorder. Intuition and the ability to think enable us to see this.

Hip! Hip! Hallelujah!

"There are winds of destiny that blow when we least expect them. Sometimes they gust with the fury of a hurricane, sometimes they barely fan one's cheek. But the winds cannot be denied, bringing as they often do a future that is impossible to ignore."
— Nicholas Sparks, Message in a Bottle

A Delicate Destiny
On The Other Hand, Missing Fingers!

Destiny is a fragile thing! Delicate! So too are dreams -- and choices! Just ask Vino! Sweet Vino! Once, long ago, he lived! Now he's dead! No one lays flowers on his grave. No one knows where it is! He simply lies there, somewhere, in an unknown, unnamed grave in the Holt Cemetery, a potter's field for the poor in New Orleans, Louisiana!

Lingering and limping through my memory – as he did through life – he turns and looks at me! I see him as I saw him as a child -- as an old man, a broken old man with missing fingers who walked on the side of his foot, limping through life. And now, the dead Vino, the old man who once lived and worked in his studio above the Old Shanty, a neighborhood bar on Washington Avenue in New Orleans – he turns and looks at me!

"I remember you," says I in the midst of the silence. "I remember you!"

Vino was an artist, a prominent European classical sculptor. Marble. Marble was his clay. He saw, chiseled and shaped beauty, freeing it from large slabs of raw marble harvested from the earth. Many of his greatest works, noble statues of great men and women of God, stand in European cathedrals – a mute testimony to a man who once was – a man who now lies buried, somewhere, in an unknown, unnamed grave in the Holt Cemetery!

"Vino died the other day," says mom. "They found him lying on his studio floor – his face half eaten away by rats!"

Marble was his clay. Alcohol was his nemesis. First the man takes a drink – then the drink takes the man! Alcohol had taken Vino where he didn't want to go! He became what he never thought he would become. Vino discovered the hard way that destiny is a fragile thing! Delicate!

Were it not for alcohol he would have been a wealthy man, a man of renown, an acclaimed man of high culture. Instead, he was scammed out of money and out of his works by shrewd art dealers and self-serving investors!

In a drunken stupor he stumbled and broke his ankle and, when he finally sobered up it was too late to reset it – and so he walked with a limp! No one knows if it was alcohol or anger that led him to chisel off several of his fingers! They were there – then they were gone! And so was his destiny! And now Vino was dead!

"Vino died the other day," says mom. "They found him lying on his studio floor – his face half eaten away by rats!"

In Numbers 13, Moses sent out 12 spies, one from each tribe, to evaluate the Promised Land. Caleb and Joshua brought back a good report concerning the land. The other 10 spies did not. Because the other 10 spies presented a bad report, the people did not want to enter the Promised Land. As a result, the Israelites, judged by God for their doubt and disbelief, wandered 40 years in the desert before they entered the Promised Land. Only Caleb and Joshua brought a good reports about the land they had seen.

For Caleb and Joshua, who eventually entered the Promised Land, Destiny was Delayed! For the 10 spies and the people of Israel who disobeyed God, Destiny was Denied! Destiny was Deferred, however, to the next generation who entered the Promised Land 40 years later.

Destiny Delayed! Destiny Denied! Destiny Deferred! Destiny's Delight!

Destiny is a fragile thing! Delicate! So too are dreams -- and choices!

> Dreams are like stars…
> you may never touch them,
> but if you follow them
> they will lead you to your destiny.
> -- Author Unknown

> It's choice, not chance –
> that determines destiny.
> -- Author Unknown

Hip! Hip! Hallelujah!

When you wish upon a star
A Single Tear Flowed Down His Cheek!

A wish is a hope or desire for something that we don't yet have. We all have hopes, dreams and desires -- wishes! John 15:7 tells us that Jesus said, "If you abide in me, and my words abide in you, ask whatever you WISH [theleo], and it will be done for you." [ESV -- English Standard Version]

The Walt Disney character -- Jiminy Cricket -- says something similar...

> *When you wish upon a star;*
> *Makes no difference who you are*
> *Anything your heart desires will come to you.*

Jiminy, is saying, "it makes no difference who you are" Anyone and Everyone Can and

Should Make A Wish; Everyone can realize their dreams -- so ask whatever you WISH!

There are many implications and many complications in life -- but, none so great that our great God cannot handle! Remember, as you "run with patience the race that is set before you…" (Hebrews 12:1), Jesus is not a Genie in a Bottle or a Genie in a Bible -- He is the Son of the Living God who says "If you abide in me, and my words abide in you, ask whatever you WISH *[theleo],* and it will be done for you. Though I did not know it then an experience I had as a child served as one of several triggers to ignite my search for Christ.

I was 11 yrs old –and an altar boy! (From "Altar Boy" to "Altar Call" – now there's a story, but, well, that's another story). I was 11 yrs old – and an altar boy! In a church! Wearing a long white robe! Lighting candles!

People, filled with fright, were suddenly, hurriedly rushing out of the sanctuary. I heard their voices but could not understand what they were saying. Then, I heard a loud sound – 'gbaam'– a small altar boy on the other side of the sanctuary carrying a golden vessel filled with incense dropped it to the cold, marble floor as he too ran from the sanctuary.

A hush of horror came over me as I quietly cowered behind several pews near the front of the church.

I could hear an angry voice shouting but it seemed far away, yet dangerously near. It was a hostile demanding voice. It was the voice of a man – a man shouting angrily! In fear, people were running from the church. I was stunned. I was shaken. The yelling and shouting voice – was getting closer and closer – to me!

"Come down from that cross! If you are the Son of God, come down from that cross!"

Above me the dying figure of Christ, carved in stone, was fastened to a large stone cross -- a huge crucifix! As I stood there, beneath the cross, cowering in fear, looking at the hard, cold chiseled face of the man, then at the hard, cold chiseled face of the stone Christ, I felt myself shaking, rocking back and forth, filled with inward trembling and fear.

The man's eyes were wild and wide with uncontrollable rage. He stared at the stone Christ, then, disorientated, half-crazed, he continued shouting angrily at the dead Christ carved in stone that hung on the cross above me. He raised one of his fists defiantly into the air, then lowered it to point an accusing finger toward the crucifix, screaming like a madman at the stone figure of Jesus.

"Come down from that cross! Come down from that cross!"

Faint and trembling, a nervous little priest wearing a long flowing black robe came into the sanctuary from behind the altar.

"Sir, please, sir. Look carefully. This Christ is but stone. He cannot hear you. He cannot come down. He is not real."

As the priest spoke, the angry man's eyes met mine. I stood motionless across from the sanctuary lamp by a rack of candles – simply staring into his eyes. Then he turned his eyes away from me and began to weep.

When the priest said "He is not real" the man looked at me again then nodded his head toward me as a single tear slowly crawled down his cheek.

Behind that tear was a hidden language whose meaning I did not then understand – I was only 11 yrs old! Only later, as an adult, would I see that tear crawl down another cheek -- my own – then I heard the language -- and understood!

When you come to the place where nothing matters -- nothing but hearing from God -- and God seems strangely silent – then you will hear – as the tear slowly crawls down your cheek -- then you will understand!

Purpose! Plan! Providence! Yes! You will understand! Trembling! Tears! Design! Destiny! Yes! You will understand!

Know this: The LORD is near, very near – and He hears your cry. He knows your heart. He sees your tears, your heartbreak, your disappointment and your pain. He knows your hopes, your passions, your desires – your wishes.

The Christ made with human hands -- the Christ made of stone, of wood, or plaster -- that Christ is not real! That Christ cannot help you.

The Christ, the Son of God, the Christ who is Very God of Very God -- He is not only high and lifted up but near, very near, and He weeps with us as we weep.

So hold on to your dreams! Hold on to your destiny! Don't give up. Don't turn back. Continue to run with patience the race that is before you.

Christ will feed your hunger. He will satisfy your thirst. He feels and is touched by your weeping and by your anguish of heart. He gathers your tears in His bottle and records them in His book. You are loved! You are remembered in heaven at the throne of God Himself (Psalm 56:8)

Unchangeable circumstances. Listen now, especially when in the midst of the unchangeable – and hear the language – and understand -- as...

A Single Tear
Slowly Crawls Down Your Cheek!

You think there's nothing out there for you, but there is. You just can't see it.
Water for Elephants

Hip. Hip. Hallelujah!

What the Blind Man Saw
Partial Obedience! Part 1

Resumes! Minister of Music.
"A dozen will be in the mail this afternoon!" So said the man at the Office of Church Minister Relations of the New Orleans Baptist Theological Seminary.

He handled resumes. We needed a Minister of Music and the seminary always seemed to have an abundance of high-quality students to serve on church staffs.

"A dozen will be in the mail this afternoon! But, could I be so bold as to recommend you consider an excellent music candidate, a phenomenal fellow actually?"
"Of course," says I.

"That's why I'm calling. If you fell that strongly about him, then send him over with his resume for an interview."

"That's the problem, sort of," says he. "If he's to be interviewed you'll have to come here to the seminary to interview him."

"What? Does he not have transportation? Is he ill or something?"

"Not quite," says he. "You see – he's blind!"

"Blind? Well, that's no problem. The steps of the righteous are ordained of the Lord. If God leads him to our church – if that's what God ordains, why, we'll be happy to have him!"

The next afternoon I sat across from and interviewed a young, blind seminarian. It was his first interview. We talked awhile about many things when suddenly, in the midst of the interview, the alarm on his wrist watch sounded. He very calmly pushed a button to silence the alarm and closed his eyes briefly as I continued talking.

"I noticed a few minutes ago that your alarm went off," says I. If you need to take medication or respond to that alarm in any way, we can stop talking for a bit."

"No. No," says he with a smile on his face. "I set my alarm to sound everyday at that hour. You see, 13 yrs ago I said 'I do' to the most wonderful woman and she said 'I do" to me. We exchanged vows and rings and kissed – I set my alarm to sound every day to remember – and I pause, pray and praise God for His special gift to me, my wife!"

"Everyday?"

"Yes, sir, everyday for thirteen years, four months and three days, to be exact."

There are some things you won't find on a resume. The blind man proved to be one of the finest Minister's of Music we'd ever had. He was blessed with a depth of spirit, a sense of worship – a simply astounding God-anointed young man!

There's a fundamental life lesson here – there is absolutely no reason not to pursue God's call – your destiny -- no matter what setbacks you encounter. Our obstacles are God's opportunities.

We should strive, strain and, yes, sometimes struggle to fulfill God's destiny for our lives! So, run with patience the race before you! God will give you strength and stamina sufficient for your need!

A second life lesson -- During one Sunday night service, when the Spirit's anointing was especially heavy, our young minister came and stood next to me. "Pastor," says he. "I have a song I wrote that I think is especially suited for this moment. With your permission I'd like to play it and sing it for our people!"

Awesome! Simply Awesome! God fell on our congregation that night! And the song – it had us soaring.

His sheet music was interesting -- roughly thirty inches in height by twenty four inches across. The music notes he had scribbled on the hand drawn super large music sheets were gigantic! Though he was blind he could see, somewhat, out of the periphery of one eye.

One final thing about that super large sheet music. At the bottom the blind musician had written an inscription……

"Partial Obedience Is Total Disobedience."

(May I say with a hush –
                      Hip. Hip, Hallelujah!)

Partial Obedience
Is Total Disobedience - Part 2

I felt the need to send a text message to a friend. For a brief few seconds I felt hesitant! Then, sensing I was being prompted of the Lord I sent it:

"Be Calm," says I.

That was the extent of the text message.
Thirty minutes later my phone rang.
"How did you know?"
"How did I know what?"
"You know, 'Be Calm!'"
"I didn't know, but He did!"

Sometimes God peeks at us and smiles through the unplanned moments of life! In that moment we may sense hesitancy but the issue is obedience.

"Partial Obedience Is Total Disobedience," wrote the blind man.

A few weeks later I was having a difficult time.

Someone sent me the following text:
"These are tender times. Just know that no matter what, God always wins. God is a big God Who can handle anything. He can handle everything. Romans 8:28 / Joshua 1:9"

Isn't it nice to have a friend like that? I don't know if my friend encountered hesitancy – perhaps yes, perhaps no! In the end, however, my friend was obedient! '

Thank you Jesus for good friends who are anointed with your tenderness, love and wisdom – friends who work through hesitancy to obedience.

Hip. Hip, Hallelujah!

The Skinny On Spiritual Warfare
There is a dark side to light

Let's begin with that which is simple, then we shall move with boldness and confidence to the more complex. Many years ago, as a young believer, I was deeply blessed as Jesus, in His providence, led me to a fresh translation of the New Testament that greatly enriched my understanding of God's purpose for my life. (Parenthetically, let me share that I highly recommend Letters To Young Churches by J. B. Phillips, a great man of God who has gone home to be with the Lord).

Time passed. I was growing in the Lord and I was being nourished by Phillips translations when Jesus led me to and blessed me with a book titled The Wounded Healer, a brief biography of J. B. Phillips, written by his wife. In the midst of the narrative of Phillips life the biographer included a prayer that Phillips had prayed. When I read that particular prayer the Holy Spirit pierced my heart. The Spirit literally gripped me, seized my attention and led me to claim that prayer and make it my own. I have prayed and do pray that prayer often with the conviction that its answer in my life and in the lives of God's children is the great need of the hour. I choose to call that prayer, though J. B. Phillips did not label it as such, "The Reality Prayer." It is a very short, very concise, simple prayer and I pray that the Holy Spirit will use it in your life as you follow Jesus.

"God, Help me to see the World as it is, Myself as I am and Thou as Thou Art."

I really believe that God is genuinely pleased when His people pray that kind of prayer. It is a prayer for truth; a simple request for the ability to understand; for discernment; for wisdom; for the gift of seeing reality unencumbered by the many illusions that distort our perceptions, cloud our understanding and hinder us in our pilgrimage through this world. I hope that you will pray that prayer and pray it often! God will hear and He will bless you.

I can say with assurance that Christ heard me as I prayed that simple prayer. I began to sense an intensification of His leadership in my life. I began to realize that we were on a pilgrimage together, Christ and me. I sensed God's call, was ordained and became a pastor. He was speaking to me, more and more as time passed, leading me deeper into and teaching me His truth. Guiding principles that would strengthen me in my walk with Him were being incorporated into my life.

He began to expose to me and quicken to me many wonderful Scriptures. For instance, in the Old Testament book of I Chronicles, chapter 12, there is a listing of King David's military companies at Zilag and his armies at Hebron. In verse 32 God spoke to me about a great need of our generation.

"The children of Issachar were men that had understanding of the times to know what Israel ought to do."

My deep conviction is that God is raising up a new generation of believers who are going to radically influence the world for Christ because He has gifted them with an "understanding of the times." They "know" what "ought" to be done and will do it! That excites me! I want to be a part of that! But, before any of us can radically influence the world our prayer should be influenced by tis simple type of prayer...

*"God, Help me see the World as it is,
Myself as I am and Thou as Thou Art."*

Now, let us move with boldness and confidence to the more complex. Lets delve a little more deeply into what I call The Skinny On Spiritual Warfare – the dark side of light.

There is a dark side to light, you know. Evil wears many disguises. It always camouflages itself as other than it is; and, good men are deceived. The very nature of deception is that the deceived do not know that they are deceived. There is a dark side to light, you know.

In all matters of faith and practice, God's Word is "a lamp unto our feet and a light unto our path." The Word of God, and the Word of God alone, can enable us to see "the World as it is."

As the Holy Spirit provides greater clarity there is one thing that becomes apparent – the World, our World -- is caught in an explosive violent spiritual conflict of cosmic proportions. Spiritual warfare, my friend, is not glamorous. No! It is dirty! It is raw! It is rough!

It spills over from one realm into the other. The spiritual and the temporal are inseparably linked, with each informing and influencing the other. There is carnage and conflict in both realms, carnage and conflict that spills over, back and forth, into one realm and then back into other!

There are casualties! The dead carcasses and bleached bones of the living dead line the spiritual roadway of life this side of heaven. Dead Carcasses? Bleached Bones? Are they not the deceived, the fornicators, the idolaters, the adulterers, the effeminate, the abusers of themselves with mankind, the thieves, the covetous, the drunkards, the revilers, the extortionists, and such like… and "such were some of you" writes Paul in 1 Corinthians 9:9-11.

No! Spiritual warfare is not a slick Hollywood production. No! It is not glamorous! There is a dark side to light. Evil wears many disguises. There is a world without color, darkened with smoke and grime. Such a place does exist, you know. I have been there – and so have you. We are there now, yes, even now. The apostle Paul calls this place, this realm, this world without color – he calls it the present evil age.

Principalities and Powers, demons and devils, evil spirits – they are infested in this dismal place. These hideous, malcontents run to and fro, back and forth, tormenting, teasing and tempting both Sons of Adam and Sons of God! There is no beauty, no color, in this realm because of their blasted infestation! They suck the color out of life – and they suck the life out of life!

Just ask the drug addict! The alcoholic! The battered wife! The abused child! Ask the one who suffers violence! The one who perpetrates violence! The angry! The hostile! The sexually abused! Just ask! Just ask! They see no glamour! No! No! A thousand times No!

Spiritual warfare is not glamorous. It never is. No! Spiritual warfare is dirty! It is raw! It is rough! Nevertheless, many, who read of spiritual warfare in the Bible – for instance, the incident of Gabriel being restrained by the Prince of Persia until Michael the Archangel joined the battle -- many read this and falsely conclude that spiritual warfare is a glorious, fantastic, spectacular battle in the heavenly realms. No! Again I say, No! It is dirty! It is raw! It is grimy – and the carnage and the violence is rageing in both the spiritual and physical realms.

What does this spiritual warfare really look like here on earth?

Here? Here, in this present evil age, is desolation! Here is desperation! Here is war! Hell contends against Heaven! Heaven rises up against Hell! Know this, "the gates of hell shall not prevail!" No! Never! Kingdom clashes against Kingdom! Spirit lusteth against flesh and flesh against Spirit!

Light does battle against Darkness! A Cosmic shattering races across the Universe! The kingdoms of this world are become the kingdoms of our Lord and of His Christ, and He shall reign for ever and ever!

Light will prevail!

Peel back the thin line that separates the temporal from the eternal, the physical from the spiritual. What do you see? An invisible war! A cosmic conflict! Eternal implications! Eternal complications! The "mystery of iniquity" unfolds, raging all around us! "And -- the kingdom of heaven suffereth violence, and the violent take it by force!" (Mt 11:12)

And God's Kingdom? God's Kingdom suffers violence? What? God's Kingdom actually suffers violence? The violent take God's Kingdom by force? You ask, "How can this be?"

Question -- who is attacking the territory of the other, Christ or Satan. If God and His church are on the offensive, then Satan and those of his realm are in a defensive posture. If Satan is on the offensive, then God and the Kingdom of Light are in a defensive posture. The difference affects how you see and how you separate the temporal from the eternal, the physical from the spiritual -- the 'world as it is' or 'the world as you think it is!'

Remember, there are three forces involved in the conflict: (1) the Divine, (2) the Devil, and, (3) the human. It would, however, be foolish, most foolish, to believe that this is a life-or-death, struggle between God and Satan. Know this: God and Satan are not engaged in or locked into a life-or-death, do-or-die, tug-of-war type of struggle. That would imply dualism, a powerful good God and a powerful evil god slugging it out. No such dualism exists. There is no such equality between God and Satan. God is God and Satan is a twerp.

When the "mystery of iniquity" happened, God removed Lucifer from his place in heaven. There was no fight between God and Lucifer. God simply spoke and it was done – "I beheld Satan as lightning fall from heaven." The struggle exists on earth because God gives man liberty, liberty as a choice as to whether a man will or will not serve God. God doesn't need man's help to defeat Satan – Satan is already defeated!

Remember the three forces involved in the conflict: (1) the Divine, (2) the Devil, and, (3) the human. Man's choice implies that the real battle is unfolding all around us, a battle for the heart of man -- and thus a large part of the battle is *within you!* And it's a dirty battle! It is raw! It is grimy – and the carnage and the violence rages… And the world, it is a world without color! An incredibly ugly, lifeless, drab place. A sad, sorrowful place – horrid and horrible -- joyless, dull -- The world without color!

> The naked truth is always better than
> the best-dressed lie
> Ann Landers

> Deep into that darkness peering,
> Long I stood there
> Wondering, fearing, doubting
> Dreaming dreams no mortal
> evere dared to dream before.
> Edgar Allan Poe

Our God (our God) is an Awesome God
He reigns (He reigns) from heaven above
With wisdom (with wisdom) power and love
Our God is an Awesome God

> Hip. Hip. Hallelujah

Shadow Games!
Casting Shadows Greater Than Ourselves

Shadow Games! We've all played Shadow Games! As children we quickly learn if we stand in a certain way – positioning ourselves in relation to Light – well, we can actually cast a shadow that is greater than ourselves! Significantly Greater than Ourselves!

In a powerfully profound way God's Christian church (that's you and me) – we – by the power of God who works in us and through us -- cast a long shadow over our culture – and our culture in turn casts a long shadow over us!

The French historian Alexis de Tocqueville once wrote, "I looked in the world and I saw the church. I looked in the church and I saw the world!"

In the ongoing battle – cultural war – we are upset about and against many things! And the battle rages on….

Flesh Against Spirit
Darkness stands in opposition against Light

We're Upset About And Against This! We're Upset About And Against That! And, We're Upset About And Against this other too!

Battered, Bloodied, and Bruised – many a weary warrior has bit into and believed several lies perpetrated in the pit of Hell. The outcome – instead of casting a shadow greater than themselves they merely shadow box – accomplishing very little as they battle unseen foes who do not exist! Know this…

God Uses SMALL People
To accomplish GREAT things

God Uses SMALL Things
To accomplish GREAT things

God Uses SMALL Places
To accomplish GREAT things

No matter how "smalls" we attach to ourselves, through Christ, our Light, we can position ourselves in relation to Light so that we can actually cast a shadow that is greater than ourselves!

It is, however, foolish to be like a man feebly stumbling in the dark while walking in the light. Jesus said "he who follows me shall not walk in darkness."

Hear me! When the eye is not single there is duplicity and the mind becomes double-minded, unstable! What saith the Scripture, "the double minded man – the duplicitous man -- is unstable in all his ways." Such a man, indeed, becomes like a man feebly stumbling in the dark while walking in the light. How sad! Truth distorted! Truth disbelieved! Illusions!

When God opens our eyes He gives us the ability to understand or at least begin to understand His gifts of discernment and wisdom. He does this so that we might see reality unencumbered by the many Illusions that distort perceptions and cloud understanding.

Yet know this: A man can have his eyes

opened, yes, even opened by the touch of God, yet still be duplicitous and not see things clearly. A man who is not legally blind can still be literally blind and not see clearly. Such was the condition of the blind man at Bethsaida. Touched by the healing hand of Jesus this blind man was given sight yet he saw "men as trees walking." He was no longer legally blind; but, he still was literally blind. He simultaneously saw yet did not see "the world as it is." He saw but did not see clearly. His vision of reality and of Truth was distorted. Where once he saw darkness now, after being touched by Christ, he saw light, but both the light and his sight were distorted. It is possible to have spiritual eyes, eyes that have been opened and yet he did not yet see clearly. Only when Jesus touches him a second time could the man say "I see all things clearly."

Know this, Christians: we who sing of God's amazing grace do sing *I once was blind, but I now see,* do not yet see all things clearly. What saith the Scripture, "For now we see through a glass darkly…"

A touch by Jesus is needed, again and again, to see things clearly.

Abraham built an altar to remember where he was first touched by God's amazing grace – "his first altar." He returned to that "first altar" again and again – seeking to be touched again and again that he might see and continue to see with greater clarity. Like the blind man he saw but needed greater clarity – that he might "see all things clearly."

Remember, the first part of J. B. Phillips' prayer was "to see the World as it is."

When you "see the World as it is" – when you see the world clearly -- you will discern and discover many things. The World is, for instance, the Devil's domain. Yes, "the earth is the Lord's and the fullness thereof;" but, the title deed to planet earth, given by God to Adam, was forfeited by Adam to that ole serpent, Satan, the Adversary.

The World is, as shared earlier, also filled with lying spirits and demons – and Illusions! The Devil has many devices and strategies in his arsenal. "We are not ignorant of his devices." He strikes at your weak points and at your strong points. He strikes at your low moments and at your high moments. He will strike at strategic people. He will strike at the down-and-out and he will strike at the up-and-coming. "Your adversary the devil, as a roaring lion," writes Peter, "walketh about, seeking whom he may devour."

I pose a rhetorical question, Where is it that he "walketh about?"

Cosmic geography is a source of contention among the inhabitants of the earth. Patterns of thinking, similarity of images, and repetition of cultural motifs distort the biblical revelation. There is a two-tiered universe with the lower tier being temporal and the upper tier being eternal. One is above, the other below. We also know that there are Heavens above the firmament, heavens below the firmament, and that there is an underworld, that region within the bowels of the earth.

I pose my question again, Where is it that he "walketh about?" In Truth our World has an inner and an outer dimension, with both sharing habitation in the lower, temporal tier. This lower, temporal tier is the domain of the Devil. The outer dimension is seen through physical sight. The inner dimension is seen through spiritual sight. These two dimensions intersect, meeting at the gloomy edge of reality. This inner world, a dark and dismal realm, is the world without color.

The Devil is the "prince of the power of the air" who "deceiveth the whole world: he was cast out into the earth, and his angels were cast out with him." Know this: He is confined to the lower tier, to the heavens below the firmament. He has access to the upper tier, which is under the aegis and authority of God, but he has no authority there. Remember, he is a defeated foe. To believe otherwise is an Illusion!

Illusion? Yes, this singular word brings us back to spiritual shadow boxing. When we lack that sense of certitude and hesitate – we need direction – direction from God!

It's easy to lose our way, to develop ambiguity and uncertainty. The writer of Hebrews cautions us to "pay attention to what we've heard…lest we drift!"

When we "drift" its usually because we've become spiritually distracted, spiritually diverted or spiritually distorted in how we see what we see.

Shadow Boxing! We've also taken a detour from what we know to be God's will and, the downward spiral begins! You stop being true to yourself, to God and quit living out God's plan for your life -- your destiny!

You may have "drifted" one step at a time, one decision at a time, one piece at a time, or at one decisive moment. If you think back, you'll find it – that moment in time when things shifted. That time when you chose to act in a way that went against what you knew to be God's plan and purpose for your life -- your destiny!

You were distracted… You diverted… You took a detour…and you disobeyed and disbelieved -- just like the 10 spies -- and you stepped away from your destiny! You chose not to pay attention to God's Voice, and now, you need a fresh word from God!

The hymnist William J. Kirkpatrick wrote the following….

> I've wandered far away from God
> Now I'm coming home;
> The paths of sin too long I've trod,
> Lord, I'm coming home.

> Coming home, Coming home
> Nevermore to roam,
> Open wide Thine arms of love
> Lord, I'm coming home.

Remember, no matter where you are you run your race, remember....

> We must pay the most careful attention therefore, to what we have heard,
> so that we do not drift away…
> --Hebrews 12:2 NI

Life without a purpose is a languid, drifting thing; Every day we ought to review our purpose, saying to ourselves, 'This day let me make a sound beginning…'
-- Thomas a Kempis

Hip. Hip. Hallelujah

Unwise Decisions!
Oh what a price we pay

When you make one -- Is there a price to pay? You know the answer to that question. Yet, we all make them Unwise Decisions!

Unwise decisions are like detours that take us away from God's plan for our lives – they cause us to "drift" away from our ultimate destination – and lead us to fail to fulfill our destiny.

When you take that kind of detour you lose your sense of direction – you no longer have a firm grasp of where you're headed – and you begin to feel a sense of hopelessness as meaningless creeps in around the edges of your life! It's not a good place to be – living in the consequence of -- Unwise Decisions!

It is then – when you're living in the consequence of Unwise Decisions -- that you need to "hear a word from God." You've "drifted" -- "wandered" – now it's time to come home!

The sad thing, quite often, is that you look back and realize that you knew you were making an unwise decision when the decision was made! You knew that your decision was an unwise decision -- but you made that decision anyway! Inexplicable! You somehow chose against yourself….against God's plan for your life…and, against God Himself – you chose against God! -- and you knew exactly what you were doing!

Know this: The lure of sin – the lure of a selfish decision -- is usually greater than the awareness of its consequence when the pressure of temptation is on!

Know this: Without exception, every time you ignore God's plan for your life a bit of His design and destiny for your life slips away.

So the next time, when you're in the Valley of Decision, pause, take a deep breath, ask yourself if the decision is in alignment with God's Plan and Purpose– His Design and Destiny -- for your life! Ask yourself, "If I am to be true to God's plan – my destiny, will this decision keep me heading in the right direction? Then, ask God to give you not only wisdom but the courage and Spirit's power to follow through in making what you know to be the right decision!

Remember, "No test or temptation that comes your way is beyond the course of what others have had to face. All you need to remember is that God will never let you down; he'll never let you be pushed past your limit; he'll always be there to help you come through it." -- 1 Corinth.10:13 The Message

Hip. Hip. Hallelujah

Some Fulfill Their Destiny
– Some Don't!

I remember him when he was a younger man. I'd heard of his powerful ministry! I'd heard his powerful preaching! And, like many other pastors I'd been inside the sanctuary of his powerful church!

His name -- Perry Sanders! Dr. Perry Sanders! He was Senior Pastor of the exciting First Baptist Church, Lafayette, Louisiana. He's in heaven now! He's in heaven!

We were long distant friends, sort of. For nearly twenty years or so we would often find ourselves on opposite sides of theological disputes, denominational conflicts, and more – but, there was something that we had that most were not aware of – a mutual respect, one for the other! Oh! We had our bouts, that's for sure, but, even in the heat of battle we spoke "the truth in love."

The last time I saw Perry was at a Louisiana Baptist Convention evangelism conference. I believe it was in Lake Charles, Louisiana. There was an invitational song being sung and I nudged my wife as a thin, frail Perry Sanders struggled to walk to the altar and then to kneel. He was kneeling and praying with one of his small grandsons as the choir and congregation sang.

As he struggled to get up he slowly walked toward my wife and me, which was strange because he was seated on the opposite side of the sanctuary.

He slowed then stopped, and simply stood before us, nodded to my wife, then, putting his hand on my shoulder, whispered in my ear, "John," said he, "I just wanted to say 'Thank You' for being a part of my life!"

Just as quickly he straightened up, looked at me – then smiled. Our eyes met, just for a second. He winked. I winked back. "Thank you." Then, he walked away. It was the last time I saw Perry.

It was not only what he said, but, how he said what he said. It was genuine, real– once again – "the truth spoken in love."

There's something special about being a part of the family of God. We're a part of one another; and, that's something to be thankful for! I am a part of you and you are a part of me!

I walked away from that experience, -- changed! I had a greater clarity about "Thanks," "Thanksgiving" and the "value" of other people.

Sometimes, when it's quiet, I think about people – and I say a little prayer – "Thank you, God, for all the people who have been a part of my life. Family. Friends. Church members. And, more, so many more!"
And, Thank you, Perry, for being a part of my life.

In life, there are many people who share our journey. There are also some extra special people who not only share our journey but shape us in ways that are deep and profound! It seems to be woven into the fabric of life that we help and influence others and others in turn help and influence us. Our lives are largely constructed using bricks handed to us by others. Even the mortar that keeps everything together – given to us!

Influence! People have a powerful influence on us! And, we have a powerful influence on them! We can encourage, cheer people on and inspire them – and they can do the same for us! On the other hand, negligence, indifference and hostility can create negative influences, one upon the other.

What about you? Discouraged? Frustrated? Hurt? Lonely? Rejected? Angry? Confused? Losing sight of your destiny? What brick and mortar have you used to build your life? And, what bricks are you handing to others as they build their lives?

Think for a moment. When I looked backward I saw Perry, and a host of others who had both positive and negative influence on me.

Who is back there, hidden in the past, perhaps unseen, casting long shadows on your life? And, who is there, before you, under the shadow of your life?

There are some big issues at play here! Things like "Rejoice" or "Regret" -- because of WHO or WHAT lingers in the shadows of your life!

Know this: Through Christ you can cast a shadow greater than yourself -- which begs the asking of one final question...

Who is under the shadow of your influence? I think we call your influence on others a "legacy!" It can be a legacy of light or...

Destiny is a fragile thing! Delicate!

So too are dreams -- and choices!
If you let people's perception of you dictate your behavior, you will never grow as a person.

Boy Meets World

Hip. Hip. Hallelujah

God Talk In Tennessee? What'd He Say???

Jonathan. His name is Jonathan. He's a Southern Gospel singer. It's his ministry and his gift from God. And, boy, can Jonathan sing. But, there's something else that's rather unique about Jonathan – his sensitivity to God's leadership!

Jonathan tells and testifies powerfully about an experience he had while doing a "gig" in Tennessee. He was winding things down and gearing up for a long ride home when God spoke.

"The Spirit of God said, 'Get thee over to Chattanooga – tonight!'" Jonathan politely told the Lord that he didn't know much if anything about Chattanooga and that he was not familiar with Chattanooga. Once again God spoke. "The Spirit of God said, 'Get thee over to Chattanooga – tonight!'"

"So I drove to Chattanooga," says Jonathan. Once in Chattanooga Jonathan shared "I didn't know what to do. I didn't know where to go. I didn't know where I was; but, God surely did! I pulled to the side of the road, only to discover that I was actually "right" where I was to be!"

Directly across from where Jonathan parked was a honky-tonk, or, as we call them in the city, a strip joint! "I went to the side door of the place," related Jonathan. "I felt led of the Lord (no trance, no vision, just led of the Lord!")

A man opened the side door; and, once again Jonathan did as he was told. "Mister," says Jonathan, "I'm a Southern Gospel singer and I don't know what in the world I'm doing here. But, here I am – and I'm sure you're going to think I'm crazy, but -- Mister, God told me to give a message to a girl named Candy. Do you have a girl named Candy who works here!"

"Ya say God sent ya', huh? Hold on I'll get her."

Jonathan was shocked. A few minutes later a young girl came to the side door. "Candy, I don't know you and you don't know me and to tell you the truth I don't even know why I'm here; but, I'm a Southern Gospel singer and God told me to ask for you BY NAME and deliver you a message. God said for me to tell you that THIS IS YOUR LAST CHANCE!

The young dancer burst into tears. "Mister," says she, "would you drive me home – to my momma and to my daddy!" And he did. As they drove to her parents home she shared that her daddy was a preacher and that she was a prodigal daughter who had left her father's house for the glitter of Chattanooga. She also shared that God revealed to her in a dream that a man she did not know would come shortly to deliver her A FINAL MESSAGE FROM GOD!

As they pulled up to the home all of the lights were on, "which was strange because it was nearly 3 a.m. in the morning," said Jonathan. Standing on the porch was a man – her daddy! As she ran from the car Jonathan said the preacher daddy gave her a giant hug then said, "Go on inside. You momma's on her knees praying for you. God told us that you were coming home tonight – we been waiting!"

Hip. Hip. Hallelujah

In John 10:27 Jesus said, "My sheep hear my voice, and I know them, and they follow me…" In Acts 16 Luke relates that Paul's missionary journey took him "to Phrygia and the region of Galatia," but they "were forbidden of the Holy Ghost to preach the word in Asia… (God told them where to go and where not to go)"

"God told me to…"
"God said that I need to…"

These statements -- and others like them – point to God's direct involvement – His personal involvement -- in the affairs of everyday life! He is intimately involved, personally involved, in the affairs of life – all the affairs of life – including my life – and your life too!

Sometimes, however, we are uncomfortable when someone says…..

"God told me to…"
"God said that I need to…

I wonder why?

We know, of course, that the Bible teaches that God is intimately and personally involved with and concerned about us – each and every one of us!

Our great God cares "if a sparrow falls to the ground" (Matt.10:28) and He is so intimate with each of us that He takes notice "if a single strand of our hair turns white (Matt.5:36). Imagine that!

And, Jesus says,
"My sheep hear my voice…"

So, why are we sometimes uncomfortable when someone says….
"God told me to…"
"God said that I need to…"

I wonder why?

I wonder why we sometimes feel uncomfortable when someone speaks this way?

These things, things of little or no consequence (sparrows, lilies of the field, our hairs, etc.), are of interest to and important to God. Remember, Jesus said that we are "valued even more than sparrows" (Luke 12:7).

Because God's Word is Truth – truth without any mixture of error – you can know this – Jesus said what He meant and He meant what He said….

"My sheep hear my voice…"

Remember, Jesus said what He meant and He meant what He said!

Henry Blackaby, Experiencing God, writes that when God invites us into some new truth or new experience…

The first crisis will be one of personal belief; The second crisis is one of tension between old patterns and new options; and the last comes in the temptation to fall back.

Can you give God a blank check?

Can you freely and with no strings attached say…

"Speak, Lord, I come to do your will,
I am ready. I am open.
Thy will is my will!

Before closing this brief conversation I don't want to make you uncomfortable, but I must simply share that I wrote this little piece for one reason and one reason only….

"God told me to…"

Hip. Hip. Hallelujah

.

No Matter What Your Lot In Life –
Build Something On It!

Jesus has certainly left His mark on history! Has He made a mark on you? Are you different because of Jesus? What about the way you think? Do you see His mark on your thinking? Has it changed? All of us are, as Tim LaHaye would say, engaged in "The Battle For The Mind [book title by LaHaye].

Many have lost that twinkle of the eye and that sparkle of a smile. They are the casualties in the battle – victimized by one of their strongest enemies – negative, sinful thought patterns! When this kind of defeat occurs you will battle with skepticism, cynicism, lustful thoughts, unbelief and doubt, and more, more, more – much more! Passivity will also surface and spiritual lethargy and inertia will begin to dominate.

Do the following…

(1) Draw a "Thought Thermometer" either on paper or in your mind to identify how Christ has (or has not) changed your thinking. (1 = little change. 10 = a lot of change) Circle the appropriate number to indicate how Christ has changed your perspective concerning money, family, work, love, forgiveness, anger, patience, sex, etc. Draw as many "Thought Thermometers" as necessary for an accurate analysis.

(2) Identify how Christ has (or has not) changed your feelings, your response to stress and your ability to cope with life. Evaluate your sense of guilt or shame on your "Thought Thermometer" (1 = little change. 10 = a lot of change) Circle the appropriate number to indicate how Christ has changed your ability to manage the emotional component of your life. Is life easier to manage since becoming a Christian? Or, is life more difficult and challenging? Rate your ability to cope, your feelings of guilt, shame, bitterness, self-image, self-esteem, personality, etc.

(3) Is there a time when you were closer to Christ than now? When was that time? What caused that closeness to change? What steps do you need to take to reclaim that closeness, and the joy and vitality you once enjoyed?

Caution: You may actually be the last person to see any real progress in your own life. And, that can be discouraging. Ask a trusted friend, your spouse, or a co-worker to answer a couple of questions for you. Explain that you are evaluating your walk with Christ and want to make it as personal as possible. Then, ask this: "What one thing would you encourage me to work on when you think of my walk with the Lord?" Then ask, "Can you point out an area or two where you feel I'm making progress?"

Enough Said!
Hip! Hip! Hallelujah!

Destiny
God has plans for you and your life!

Through the prophet Jeremiah (29:11 MSG) God says, "I know what I'm doing. I have it all planned out--plans to take care of you, not abandon you, plans to give you the future you hope for."

You may think that God has nothing planed for you -- but He does! You may feel that God is busy working out His plans for others, but not you – stinkin' thinkin' – know this… God has plans for you and your life!

And it's not just a hastily drawn up plan! It's a plan to give you a good and prosperous future – the kind of future you hope for!

No matter where you are in life, remember…

God has plans for you and your life!

A number of years ago my wife and I enjoyed an evening at a local restaurant. When the young waiter brought the check I felt led to write a little note on the receipt, a note just for him (I do that sometimes – when God tells me to). The note was a simple note…

God has plans for you and your life!

Several weeks later my wife and I visited the same restaurant. The same young waiter eagerly shared how grateful he was for the note!

"I was down in the pits, feeling like a loser. I had just graduated from college, unable to find a job in my field – banking – I took this job serving tables. My mom has been praying for me. She was worried. I was worried. Everybody was worried. I was down in the pits, feeling like a loser….all those years of studying banking….

'Then I got your note. It was as if God was speaking – to me! I called my mom immediately and told her – 'Mom! God has plans for me and my life! God has plans for me and my life!'"

"How do you know," asked his mom?
"God sent me a note," says he.

A few weeks later we visited the same restaurant again!

"He quit," says the boss. "Got a job as a banker in the city!"

I remember the young waiter shared he wanted to go into banking -- that was his major in college. God's plans were evidently unfolding!

About three years later my wife and visited a different restaurant.

"New Ownership" – read the sign in front of the building.

A familiar looking waiter came with the menu.

"You don't remember me. Years ago you left me a little note! *God has plans for you and your life!* I own this place!"

Prologue

Do you ever wish life
had a "redo" feature?

Do you ever wish life
had a "restore" feature?

Do you ever wish life
would give you a "mulligan?

Bad News -- Life doesn't work that way!
Good News –God Does!

There's a new day coming! Our past failures are not final and our pain need not be fatal!

Know this -- your yesterdays don't always have to determine your tomorrows!

Hip. Hip.
Hallelujah!

www.ingramcontent.com/pod-product-compliance
Lightning Source LLC
Chambersburg PA
CBHW071752080526
44588CB00013B/2223